HOW TO USE

EVERNOTE

FOR WRITING & RESEARCH

. . . .

. . . .

NANCY HENDRICKSON

HOW TO USE EVERNOTE
FOR WRITING & RESEARCH

WHO AM I AND WHY DID I WRITE THIS BOOK?

I'm both a self-published and traditionally published author, who maintains a fulltime writing business. I write about topics as diverse as self-publishing, writing, history, genealogy, and technology. When not writing, I'm off building WordPress websites or photographing the frontier west.

Because I work on so many different projects and for such a variety of clients, I quickly discovered the need to organize all of my research and writing in one place. As I no longer keep paper files, I needed a service that replicated the ease and organizational structure of a filing cabinet and hanging files. Evernote was that service. But in all honesty, I didn't immediately embrace it. It took about six months of stops and starts before I realized just how big a difference Evernote made – not only in researching a book or a project, but also in the writing process.

Since creating Evernote folders for all of my current and future projects, I no longer have to search through a stack of paper to find the exact piece of information I need. And I'm not stumbling around the Internet, trying to re-find valuable sites I hadn't bothered to bookmark.

Today, Evernote is my go-to online service for stashing ideas for blog articles, ideas for new projects, client meeting notes, marketing thoughts, web clippings, contracts, and notes about each project. Not to mention audio notes and video clips I've created.

Because it's not unusual for me to come up with a new book idea while still working on a current project, Evernote gives me the luxury of keeping all of my notes in one – very organized – location. Once you start using Evernote, I doubt that you'll ever return to paper.

In this book, I've done my best to introduce you to the magic of Evernote – and more importantly how you – the writer – can make it your default research and writing assistant.

May I Gift You This Guide?

As my way of saying thanks for purchasing this book, I'd like to give you a step-by-step guide to IFTTT.com – a site that allows you (for free) to set up a "domino effect" social media marketing plan with ease. I call it One-Click Marketing because you really can post book promotions on multiple sites, all from a single post or image.

http://nancyhendrickson.com/free

Here's what one reader emailed me:

"I first ran across IFTTT in a blog on Sunday. Went to the site. Yikes! Thought another shorthand communication system that I can't understand. Then I downloaded your guide. You validated the whole IFTTT concept. Thank you!!"

Jeff Ezell

CONTENTS

LIST OF ILLUSTRATIONS

WHAT IS EVERNOTE®?

With a floppy-eared elephant for a logo and a tagline of 'Remember Everything,' it's pretty clear what Evernote is all about. In a nutshell, Evernote is about saving 'stuff'. And by stuff, I mean documents, text, websites, images, video, and audio. In short, everything you don't want to forget to remember.

Because Evernote is a multi-platform system, all of your stuff can be synced between devices (desktop, tablet, phone), giving you easy access to important (or not so important) documents whether you're at home, in the office, or on-the-go. Evernote is freely available for both Windows and Mac computers, the iPhone, iPad, Android, and other smart devices.

If you're a writer of any genre – or even someone who only occasionally writes (biz folks, students, etc.), Evernote is the nearly perfect system. Or, as my Mary Poppins-loving friends would say: "Practically perfect in every way."

Evernote's features are many, its add-ons are useful, and its apps are growing in number. Basic (free) features include:

- ➤ Emailing notes directly to Evernote
- ➤ Creating and organizing Notebooks for each project
- ➤ Storing information you've found online
- ➤ Sharing notes to your social media profiles
- ➤ Sharing a notebook with collaborators
- ➤ Creating PDFs or a slideshow of notes
- ➤ Easily searching notes and images via a powerful in-system search tool
- ➤ Tagging notes for easy searching
- ➤ Setting up reminders
- ➤ Increasing day-to-day productivity
- ➤ Creating checklists
- ➤ Importing scans
- ➤ Capturing ideas
- ➤ Setting geolocations
- ➤ Storing source URLs

WHY USE EVERNOTE?

I don't know about you but, unless I write something down, in a day or two (or 10 minutes) my brilliant idea has migrated to the Lost Ideas section of my brain. Kinda like socks in a washer.

And wouldn't you know it, when an idea strikes I'm usually away from my desk, scrambling to find a scrap of paper for my scribbles. And once I've jotted an idea on the back of an envelope, how good a job do you think I do in organizing and archiving *that* note? Right.

While online archive services like Dropbox are excellent for backing up important files, Evernote has become my go-to virtual assistant when working on a book or client project because I can just click and automatically add a note to the appropriate folder. Even better (at least for me) Evernote and Siri make for a fantastic team. More on that later in the IFTTT Chapter.

> **NOTE:** *The word 'Note' is Evernote's default name for anything you put into a folder. So when I use the word 'note', know that I mean any media (audio, video, etc.).*

Before setting up your account and digging into Evernote's bones, let me say a word or two about how I use Evernote – and how it's upped my productivity.

Right now, I store:

- ➢ Writing prompts
- ➢ Inspirational images
- ➢ Ideas for my next book
- ➢ Outline of my current book
- ➢ Interviews

- ➢ Ideas to send my book cover designer
- ➢ Ideas I want to send to my email list
- ➢ Screenshots
- ➢ Images for my blog
- ➢ To-do list
- ➢ Word documents
- ➢ Saved Google searches
- ➢ Scanned business-related receipts
- ➢ Trip notes
- ➢ Trip specifics (reservations, hotels, etc.)
- ➢ Research
- ➢ Web clippings

Sitting in Evernote are all of the things I used to keep on scraps of paper or as an image on my phone - all unorganized. Not anymore.

Fortunately for those of us who research and write, Evernote built its foundation on a system of Notebooks and Notes. If you're used to saving documents on your hard drive, Notebooks and Notes is akin to Folders and Files.

If this is your first time using Evernote, these are the basics you'll need to know to really rock the system:

NOTEBOOKS

Notebooks are the repository for major topics, big ideas, book projects, clients, etc. With the basic version of Evernote (free) you can create up to 100 different notebooks.

Some people start off using Evernote by just creating notes and not using notebooks. For me, that takes away the advantage of being uber-organized so create notebooks first. Then add more as needed.

NOTES

Within each notebook are Notes. Notes can be in just about any format, including text, audio, video, and photos. Each time you create a note, specify the notebook in which to stash it and – boom! – you're organized. You can even drag and drop notes from your computer directly into a notebook.

Remember what I said about Siri and Evernote? I can open Evernote, tap for a new note, and use my iPhone microphone instead of the keyboard to create a note. When I'm done, the note is automatically converted to text. This works really well for me because I'm in the car so much (meetings, meetings, meetings). It may be a feature you never use – but try it, and I'm pretty sure you'll be hooked.

Don't be jealous Android-user. You, too, have the speech to text option. Tap to open a new note, then tap the 'speech to text' icon (it looks like a quote bubble with a microphone inside of it) then start talking. Evernote will automatically convert the speech to text and compose a new note, and it will also save and attach your voice recording to the text input.

DO YOU NEED FREE OR PREMIUM?

Evernote comes in basic (free) and premium versions. By default, you'll get the free version, which I think is all you'll ever need for writing or research projects. I suppose there may be times when you might need to upgrade to premium service but to date, I haven't come close to needing it.

Here's what Premium offers you that you can't get in basic:

- ➤ Monthly uploads of 1GB per month vs. basic's 60MB
- ➤ Ability to access offline notebooks (great for travelers who can't get a wifi connection)
- ➤ Top priority support
- ➤ Collaborative editing of notes[1]
- ➤ Notebooks can hold up to 100MB vs. basic's 25MB
- ➤ Pin lock: iOS and Android users can add a lock for security
- ➤ PDF search: Evernote can search through your scanned PDFs

Premium Evernote currently costs $5 a month or $45 a year.

---

[1] *The shared access and editing to previous notes is an excellent feature when multiple people are working on the same project. Notes that have been stored or saved can be edited by other people, once permission has been granted. As long as each party has access to the internet, such changes can be made successfully.*

FIRST STEP:
SET UP YOUR ACCOUNT

Go to Evernote.com and follow the directions to create an account using your email address and creating a password.

Once your account is live, download the **desktop version** for either Windows or Mac. Click the downloaded file and follow the on-screen instructions to install the program. You'll need to check your email to verify your email address for registration. Read and agree to the Terms and Conditions. Once Evernote is installed and launched, sign in using your email and password.

If you happened to miss the desktop download screen, go to this page:

http://evernote.com/products

and in the right column you'll find links to download Evernote for Windows desktop and phone, iOS, Blackberry, Mac, and Android.

You can also download Evernote for your mobile devices. Go to:

https://evernote.com/evernote

and, from the dropdown box, select the computer or device that you want to install.

SYNCING BETWEEN DEVICES

Before going any further, I want to introduce you to one of Evernote's most useful features (in my opinion) – the ability to sync all information across all of my devices. For me, that means full access on my PC, iPad, and iPhone. On the PC Desktop version, you can click the Sync link on the top menu. Or, if you want to define how often Evernote syncs, click Tools on the menu bar, then Options.

From the Option box, click the Sync tab. From here you can set Evernote to sync every 15 or 30 minutes, every hour, or every day.

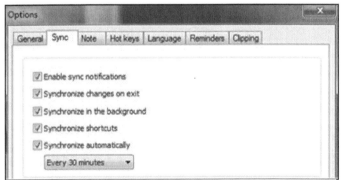

Screenshot 1: Sync options

On your mobile device, tap the refresh (sync) icon to instantly start a new sync.

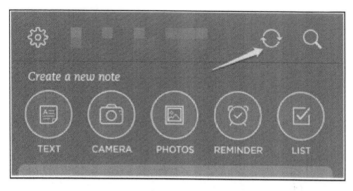

Screenshot 2: Refresh (Sync) options

My preferred device usage (which may vary greatly from your own) are:

- ➢ Online Evernote
- ➢ iPhone Evernote
- ➢ Desktop Evernote

However, whichever version you choose to use as your primary one, everything you do will still be accessible on all of your devices. The more you use Evernote, the more you'll appreciate this feature.

NAVIGATING THE HOME SCREEN

If you're using the online version of Evernote (which I most often use – primarily because I do so much online research) this section will walk you through navigating the system.

Desktop and mobile versions vary slightly but, once you understand the basics, you won't have any problems using Evernote on any device.

When you log into your home screen online you'll see that it's comprised of three columns. (Screenshot is of my Evernote account on the Web.)

Screenshot 3: The 3 columns of the home screen

By the way, do you like the cool arrows and labels on this image? I created it using an Evernote property – Skitch[2]. It's available as a free desktop download for Windows and Mac, as well as iOS and Android devices.

LEFT COLUMN

Shortcuts

Use shortcuts to quickly find the things you use most often. You'll find the Shortcuts section above the Notebooks section.

---

[2] http://evernote.com/skitch

Add a shortcut by dragging notes, a notebook, or tags into this section of the page.

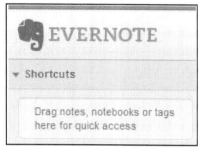

Screenshot 4: Shortcuts

Notebooks

You'll see a list of all of your Notebooks listed in alphabetical order. You'll also see a number next to the Notebook name; this denotes the number of notes within that specific Notebook.

Stacks

If you create a notebook (let's say it's titled "Baseball") and you want to also create notebooks for each team that are stored under the main notebook "Baseball," this collection of related notebooks is called a Stack.

Scroll down below the name of the notebooks to find a list of Tags that have been created. (More on Tags later.)

MIDDLE COLUMN

The center of the page is where you'll see a list of all notes within a selected notebook.

RIGHT COLUMN

Tags

Select any note and above the note you'll see any tags that were assigned to the note. A list of all tags can be found on the left side of the screen as noted earlier.

Note Contents

On the right side of the screen, beneath the tags you'll see the contents of your note.

Title

The system will create a default title for your note, based on the first line of the note. Highlight the note (middle column) to enable editing of the title.

CREATE A NOTEBOOK

You **can** create notes without creating a notebook, but at some point you'll want to organize notes by notebook. So why not go ahead and create notebooks first?

Although you can find loose notes using the Search function, you'll quickly see that starting with notebooks will make your life much easier. If you don't bother creating notebooks, three months from now you'll smack yourself in the head and say, "What was I thinking?"

Notebooks take two seconds to create and once created, they ensure that all of your notes relating to a certain topic are kept in the same place.

HOW CAN A WRITER BEST USE NOTEBOOKS?

The possibilities are almost endless:

- ➢ Book outline
- ➢ Fiction book research (top of the stack)
- ➢ Place research (part of the stack)
- ➢ History research (part of the stack)
- ➢ Character notes (part of the stack)
- ➢ Writing prompt images
- ➢ Interviews
- ➢ Inspiration (usually images)
- ➢ New book ideas
- ➢ Great quotes
- ➢ Websites with relevant information (think: wiki)
- ➢ Copyright-free images
- ➢ Invoice reminders
- ➢ Project to-do lists
- ➢ Deadlines
- ➢ Query letters
- ➢ Website updates

- ➢ Mailing list ideas
- ➢ Blog topic ideas
- ➢ Random ideas to explore
- ➢ Articles on the craft of writing
- ➢ Books to read
- ➢ Writing tidbits (line of dialogue, character description, action idea)

If you're writing and / or researching for business or school, you'll have different categories, trending more towards expenses, travel, documents, product research, receipts, mileage, car rentals, classes, assignments, etc.

HOW TO CREATE A NOTEBOOK

Click the New Notebook button and then name the notebook. If you change your mind about the name, right click the notebook name and choose the Rename option.

As a quick reminder - **Stacks** are comprised of a major topic with sub-topics. Think of them like this:

FRUIT

banana

orange

apple

pear

blackberry

To create a Stack, right click on the first notebook that you want to add to a stack. In this case, right-click 'banana'. One of your options will be (duh) Add to Stack. If this is your first stack, click New Stack. Name the new stack (Fruit) and from here on, anytime you want to add a notebook to a stack, just right click the notebook and the pop-up box will give you the name of all the stacks that you've created.

In this screenshot, you can see that I have the option to add a notebook to a stack titled Expenses or to a stack titled W.S. Book, or, I can also create a new stack.

Screenshot 5: Add to stack

If you decide to delete a stack the good news is that it will not delete the notes or the notebooks within the stack. The only thing that happens is the notebooks will be removed from the stack and placed back into the alphabetical list of all of the notebooks. You can also drag and drop one notebook onto another to create a stack.

> **HINT** *If you use an underscore (i.e. _) at the beginning of the notebook name, it will appear at the top of your alphabetical list. Notebook name would look like this:*
>
> ## *_Idea File*
>
> *I typically use this naming convention for my most current book project because I like to see it at the top of the list.*
>
> *If you've already named a notebook and now you want to add the underscore, right click the notebook name and select the Rename option.*

CREATE A NOTE

Click on 'New Note' on the top bar – it's to the right of the search box. Give the note a title and then click your cursor into the text box below the title.

Once you do this, a new editing bar will appear. The editing bar has all of those familiar icons you see in your word processing program. These include italics, bold, underline, bullets, alignment, font, font size, and font color.

You'll also find two additional tools in the editing bar that you may not be familiar with: Checkboxes and Tables.

The checkbox creates... well, checkboxes – great for list-making. The table tool inserts a table, with user-specified number of rows, columns, and width. Width can be defined in percentage of page or pixels.

If you use the checkboxes for a list, you can actually click in the box and it will automatically add a checkmark. Click a second time to remove the checkmark.

ADD AN ATTACHMENT TO A NOTE

Want to add an attachment to your note? Click the paperclip in the editing toolbar.

If you attach a document, you'll see a paperclip in the body of your note along with the name of the file. If you attach an image, the image itself will be in the note's body. In this image, you can see checkboxes, an image, and a document – all as part of the same note.

Screenshot 6: Add an attachment to a note

NOTE SHARING

With the basic (free) service you can share a note via SMS Message, Twitter, Facebook, and via email. With the premium service, the people with whom you share can also edit your note. You can also copy the link to the note and share it in the same ways.

NOTE MERGING

This is a wonderful feature and one I frequently use. Let's say you're going to write a new book on how music of the 1960s differs from music of the 1970s. You've captured a lot of notes and web sources for your book but now you'd like to get all of those notes into a single document that you can download and use as your primary reference.

To merge notes, select the notes you want to merge (Command + Click on Mac or Ctrl + Click on PC). A thumbnail of all of the notes will appear in the Note Viewer (right column). Click the Merge button. How cool is that. As you can see from the image on the next page, you can also email the merged notes.

Continental Railroad

research continental
railroad compare accuracy
with Hell on Wheels find
period book about the
railroad

5 Notes Selected

| Merge | Email | Delete |

Copy Note Links to the Clipboard

Move to notebook ▼

Add Tags... | Add

Screenshot 7: Merging & emailing notes

EMAIL A NOTE TO EVERNOTE

I love this feature, and I'm dying to tell you why.

I read many blogs and news sources every morning on my iPad using the Flipboard app (available for Android and iOS). My Flipboard and my coffee get me out the door for my walk.

Every day, I run across news items that I might use in some future project – or they have some wonderful resource that I don't want to lose.

Using Evernote, you can email them directly into your account, along with tags and specifying the notebook. If you don't know your Evernote e-mail address, go to the Account Info area of Evernote for Windows and Mac, Settings on Evernote Web, and the Sync tab on Evernote for iPhone and iPad — your Evernote email will be listed there. On an Android device, go to Settings then Account Info to find your Evernote email. Add the address into your contact list or address book.

In the screenshot on the next page, you can see that I found a great article about mailing lists on Jane Friedman's site (via Flipboard on my iPad). I emailed it directly into my Evernote account using the Evernote-assigned email address.

If you want the note to go to a specific notebook, append the subject line with the symbol "@" followed by the name of an existing notebook. To add a tag, include "#" followed by an existing tag.

DELETING A NOTE

Deleting a note is simple. Select the note from the note list in the middle column. On the far right side of the editing toolbar you'll see the trashcan icon. Select the icon to delete the note.

Screenshot 8: Emailing to Evernote

Oh-oh. Did you delete a note by mistake? No worries. You can find it in the left column inside the notebook titled 'Trash'. From the Trash notebook select the note you want to un-delete. In the right column you'll now see your note with two options above it: Restore or Delete (permanently).

This note is in the trash. You cannot edit it unless you restore it   Restore Note   Delete Note

Screenshot 9: Deleting a note

HOW TO ADD AUDIO NOTES

Not all of the notes you save into Evernote need to be text. If you prefer to dictate audio notes and then listen to them later, that capability is well within the power of the Evernote program. Recording audio notes is easy and, once recorded, they can be filed and organized just as any other note within your account. This is a great tool to use when you just want to get out a bunch of ideas or information that has been in your head – but you don't want to type it all out.

For authors, audio notes are particularly useful when working on a creative story that might lead in many different directions. As you work your way through the story, various ideas and directions may pop into your head at any time. No matter where you are, it will only take a few seconds to record an audio note that you can access later when you are actually working on the project.

How to Use Audio Notes

As with almost every function in Evernote, recording an audio note is simple to do once you've done it a time or two. If you're recording a note on your desktop or laptop computer, you'll need a microphone connected to the computer.

The desktop version of Evernote has a pulldown menu under New Note; from here you can create an audio note, ink note (see next section), webcam note, a text note, or a new screenshot.

Screenshot 10: Creating an audio note

Click the New Audio Note menu option, then the Record option at the top of the right column.

Screenshot 11: Recording an audio note

If you like, you can even type into the note at the same time that you are recording. When finished, just save the audio to your note and you're done. The note can be moved around like any other note within your Evernote account, so you can put it in the appropriate notebook and tag it with any relevant words.

If you are using a mobile device, either iOS or Android, you can still use the audio recording feature. On iOS, open up a note and tap on the microphone icon. It's pretty small so I captured a screenshot to show you which icon is the mic.

Screenshot 12: The mic icon

By the way, Skitch has a pixelating feature that I used in the mic icon image – it pixelated out my address. Handy, eh?

Once you tap the mic, just start recording.

For Android, you will tap on the '+' icon after you open a note, and then tap 'record audio' to get started. If you are using a free Evernote account, you can record notes up to 25MB in size, while premium users are able to go up to 100MB. The length of an audio file that can be recorded under those limits depends greatly on the type of audio that you are recording, as well as what kind of device you happen to be using.

Ideas for Audio Notes

I already discussed a little about how to use audio notes to capture stray ideas. However, they're also great to use once you sit down and start working on a project. A few ideas are:

INTERVIEWING A SOURCE

If you're using a variety of sources to pull together information for your project, you can use the audio notes feature to record an interview. Two things to keep in mind: 1) Make sure you have the other person's permission to record your conversation. For legal reasons, it might be best to get that permission in writing; 2) Make sure you test out the length limitations of recording notes on your device before using it during an interview. You don't want to run out of space in the middle of a valuable interview. That's the digital version of dead batteries.

REMEMBER MUSIC

Have you ever found yourself in a situation where you hear some music (live or on the radio) and it connects you to a specific feeling or emotion that you want to journal about or try to recreate in words? If you think quickly, you can create an audio note to remember the music and hopefully connect you back to the feelings. I like this idea and have just started experimenting with it. Let me know what you think.

DICTATE INSTRUCTIONS TO YOURSELF

When you know you're going to be away from your desk and running lots of errands or going to a new address for the first time – just do a quick audio note to make sure you haven't forgotten anything on your list. Bank, post office, bookstore... You know: all the normal stuff.

You know, if your life is like mine, my tolerance and proficiency at writing out notes has drastically decreased. Evernote's audio note feature is just one of those must-have tools in my author arsenal.

CREATE A WEBCAM NOTE

As with audio notes, select the Webcam Note from the New Note pulldown. You can add a screenshot or a webcam photo to your note using Evernote's Windows version.

I like this idea for taking a quick shot of you holding your new book and then sharing it with people who are helping you promote.

A box will pop up where you'll be able to see a preview and choose which webcam to use or if you want to do a screen capture instead. Click on "Take Snapshot." If you're happy with the image, go ahead and save it to Evernote and edit your note. Otherwise, you can retake the snapshot.

CREATE AN INK NOTE

The Windows version of Evernote lets you create Ink Notes using drawing tools. This way you can actually create a handwritten note or use Ink Notes to create diagrams, shapes, and even doodles.

Like Audio Notes, select Ink Notes from the New Notes pulldown box, add the title of your note, and start writing with the pencil tool via your mouse. You can change the line thickness and color as well as cut out part of the image or your words by using the cut tool.

Honestly, I'm really terrible at this kind of note and it frustrates me to the point that I don't use it. However, you may have far more skills than I do in using your mouse to draw something. If I had a graphics tablet, I'd probably use this feature a lot. By the way – you can move elements in your drawing around by choosing the dotted rectangle tool and then drawing a circle around the element you want to move.

CREATE AN IMAGE NOTE

Do you ever take photos on your mobile device, only to forget they are even sitting in your gallery waiting to be viewed? As easy as it is to snap a picture, it's just as easy to forget you ever took it. Using Evernote, you can save images into your notebooks for later retrieval.

How can an author use images that deserve to be saved as notes? Find a book in the library that has a page you wish to reference for your project. Or, take a picture of your printer cartridge so you know what to buy the next time you're at the office supply store. Or, snap photos of a whiteboard at a meeting.

Perhaps above all else, integrating Evernote on your mobile device is a great opportunity to capture inspiration whenever it strikes. One of the most important abilities that a writer can have is to grab great ideas before they can slip away – and if you're like me, oftentimes my inspiration comes in the form of an image.

Getting Images into Evernote

If you are going to keep your important images in Evernote, you need to be able to get them into your account quickly and easily. Fortunately, there are plenty of ways to do that. Images can be placed right into your notes, and those notes can be put into any notebook that you wish. Organization is what Evernote is all about, and that is certainly true of the way it can help you maintain order within a sea of images.

IMAGES ON YOUR COMPUTER

If you have pictures that are already on your computer and you would like to add them to Evernote, the process is very simple. All you will need to do is open a note within Evernote (either a new note or an existing one), and add the image into the note. You can drag the image into the note or open the paperclip icon and load the image file that way.

IMAGES ON YOUR MOBILE DEVICE

There is a good chance that you use your smartphone as your main camera, so most of your pictures are probably saved on it. Using the Evernote app on your mobile device, you can use much the same process to add your images to a note. Once inside a note, you can tap either the camera icon or the paperclip icon and add your photo. It's possible to add existing photos to a note or to take a new photo and save it directly to Evernote.

Once images are saved into your notes, you can annotate them to save ideas, remember specifics portions of the image that you found interesting, or any other purpose you can think of.

Make Your Images Searchable

One of the biggest problems with just keeping your images on your desktop computer – or stored within your phone – is that you can't really search through them very effectively. Sure, you can look at them in chronological order, but that's about it. As the quantity of images you have saved starts to climb, you're going to have a harder and harder time finding exactly the photo you want.

Evernote is such a powerful tool in part because it can make just about anything searchable. It's up to you to best utilize this capability by logging your images in a logical manner. Adding tags to the notes that contain your images is a great way to make them easy to find. For example, imagine that you are writing a book about puppies. You have taken countless images of all sorts of adorable puppies, and you need to store them logically to use later.

Adding tags to these images will make them far easier to find when the time comes. Tags like 'short haired,' 'white hair,' 'golden retriever,' 'large dogs,' 'floppy ears,' and countless more can make your photo notes all that much easier to sort through. If you are consistent in your tagging of the images right from the start, it will only take typing in the tag into the search engine on Evernote to reveal all related images.

Additionally, text within images is also searchable (as long as it is legible). This is an incredible feature and lets you sort through images that have words in them without even applying the proper tag – although you should still tag them. Searching the text within an image might not be a function that you use on a regular basis – but it can be a lifesaver when you really need it.

TAKING PHOTOS OF NOTES

Even in a digital world, lots of writers (like me) still like to jot notes by hand. For some of us, the act of writing by hand is part of the creative process. However, at some point those ideas need to make their way into the computer so they can become part of your written work. If you have piles of notes stacked up all around your desk, it might be time to get them saved in digital form for both convenience and safety.

Rather than re-typing all of your notes into a word processing document, simply snap photos of them and save them into Evernote notes for later use. You can tag all of these images so they are organized neatly, and your text within the images may even be searchable – depending on how clearly your notes are written. What would have once been a day-long job (transcribing written notes) can be done in just minutes thanks to your smartphone and the Evernote app.

Even though we authors use words as our main mode of communication, images still play a vital role in almost every writing process. No matter what kind of project you're working on, it's a good bet that you are referencing images in one manner or another along the way. Evernote makes it quite simple to save and access the photos that are most important to your project. By establishing a logical tagging system and getting all of your images stored into Evernote notes and notebooks, you can know that they will always be just a couple of clicks away.

How you can use images and Evernote is something I'm exploring more and more every day. Would love to hear how you integrate the two: [nancy@nancyhendrickson.com].

SKITCH – HOW TO USE THIS FREE MARKUP UTILITY

As mentioned earlier, Skitch is an Evernote property that is available for desktop download or for digital devices. In brief, Skitch has several tools that you can use with your images. These include pixelating (blurring), adding arrows, text, a box, pencil tool, and a stamp (smiley face, frowny face, etc.).

I love using Skitch to either give someone directions, annotate a map, to illustrate a point that's hard to make without arrows, or to point out icons or menus on a website – just like I've done in this book.

Here's another use for Skitch: not long ago, someone asked me what a 'ray system' and a 'sea' was on the moon. It was easy for me to pull up one of my moon photos and use Skitch to point out the system. (Did you know my first two books were on astronomy?)

More on Skitch: If you blog, you can use Skitch to capture screenshots or grab images that you can crop, annotate, or pixelate. And, the screenshots you capture

with Skitch are full-text searchable. Any image you screenshot in Skitch and add to Evernote will automatically be searchable.

Screenshot 14: Highlighting things with Skitch

This comes in really handy if you screen capture a webpage and you want to make certain you can find a specific word or phrase when doing an Evernote search.

SHARING A NOTEBOOK

Now that you know how to create notebooks and notes, I want to cover how to share a notebook.

You may be wondering why you'd ever want to do this. Well, you may be collaborating on a project, co-authoring a book, you may want to run an idea by a friend or colleague, or you may want to share your writing portfolio with a prospective client.

NOTE: If you want to use Evernote as an online portfolio, save any pertinent work such as ~~content,~~ cover ~~cover of~~ your ~~document.~~ it way to sha ~~tive or~~ curren

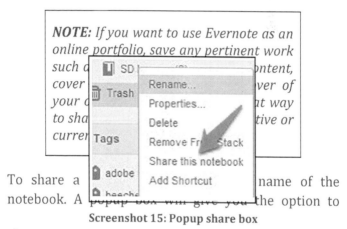

To share a ~~notebook~~ name of the notebook. A ~~popup box will give you~~ the option to share.

Screenshot 15: Popup share box

Once you click Share this notebook, you'll get another box that gives you the option to share the notebook with the public or to share with an individual.

In this case, you'd want to share with an individual. Click the appropriate link and yes, you'll get one more box.

Screenshot 16: Sharing a notebook

This box alerts you to (A) the name of the notebook that you're sharing; (B) whether to allow the person to access the notebook without logging into Evernote;

and (C) a place where you can leave a personal note. You can enter multiple email addresses by putting a comma between each address.

Notes and Notebooks Take-Away

Now that you know how to create notes and notebooks, I want to share a few thoughts about how we writers can utilize the two.

As you begin to amass notes I think you'll see how logical it is to use notes to create an outline. The more notes you pull into Evernote, the more apparent that what you're really doing is collecting book or article topics. For example, let's say you're writing a book about planning a road trip. And your notes are web clippings about maps, locations, interviews, restaurants, hotels, reward programs, airline miles, etc. In a very short time, you'll have enough notes to actually create the book's outline.

Regardless of what you're writing, I suggest including an 'Ideas' notebooks. This is where you can throw everything that crosses your mind but doesn't have a firm place to live. For me, that notebook holds ideas for future books, a sentence I know I want to use somewhere, an image that I think I want to include in a book, a possible idea about a trip... All those things that aren't definitive enough to warrant a notebook of their own.

THE POWER OF TAGS AND REMINDERS

Some of the basic features of Evernote can end up being the most useful and the most powerful. This is how I feel about tags and reminders. If you aren't taking advantage of both the tagging system and the reminders, you're not harnessing Evernote's power. The beauty of both of these features is that they are easy to use and are time-savers. Good news for the productivity crowd.

Tags, Tags, Tags

If you use WordPress as your blogging platform, you're already familiar with tags. Anytime you create a blog post you have the option to add tags, which give the post some SEO (search engine optimization) oomph.

If you're not using WordPress, tags are words or short phrases that are associated with the topic of your note. If I wrote a blog post about dealing with a bad book review, my tags might be 'book review,' 'bad book review,' 'self-esteem,' 'how to deal with trolls.'

In terms of Evernote, using tags makes it easier to search through all of your content because the system can search through all of your **notebooks by tag name**.

Here's a foodie example. You've just created a note into your Evernote account that lists great restaurants and hotels in Seattle (for an upcoming travel book). Tags could be 'Seattle,' 'fine dining,' 'five star hotels,' and more. As your Evernote archives grow and you accumulate notes full of travel tips, you can search through the notes using any of the tags you just created.

A simple search of the 'Seattle' tag will bring up any of the notes that you have tagged with that word, regardless of which notebook they're in. Instead of searching through all of your content for the travel book, all Seattle-relevant notes will be quickly found – with results displayed in the middle column.

One more thing about tags and yes, I'm still on the foodie example. If you're writing a cookbook that has a lot of baking recipes, you could add the tag 'cookie' to every recipe idea relating to cookies. Why do this? It's possible that the recipe note will not include the word 'cookie', AND it's possible that the word 'cookie' may not be mentioned within the recipe itself. Not likely, but it's possible. If this is the case, then a search for the word 'cookie' won't pull up any results. However, if you've tagged it, Evernote will find it.

Tagging a Note

Simply select 'Click to Add Tags' when you're working on your desktop or laptop computer. On iOS devices, click the "i" information icon then add tags.

Screenshot 17: Adding tags on iOS devices

For Android, you will need to select 'tags' on the top bar of the note. The exact tags are up to you – create ones that are easy to remember and that will come in handy on many of your future projects. This way you can develop a useful database of information.

That last paragraph was really important – so just in case you skimmed over it: If you write a lot of books or magazine articles or blog posts or web content and you generally write about the same topic, listen up. **By using tags you can find all of the related content for your next project** and easily pull source material or research over into your new project. Here's an example:

I wrote a book about iOS photography apps. Photo apps serve a variety of purposes so each app has its own set of tags. If I tag an app with 'filters,' that's my code for remembering that the primary feature of that app is the ability to add a bunch of filters to a photo. Why do I care? Because once I'm done with the writing process, I can then search all of my photo app tags and arrange the content of the book around the most important benefit of an app. This way each chapter of the book will contain the apps with a specific feature.

One common mistake that some Evernote users make is assuming they won't ever have enough notes in their account to justify the use of tags, so they neglect to add them to their notes. As time passes and their notebooks get bigger and bigger, they suddenly wish they would have taken a few extra seconds to add tags when the note was created.

REMINDERS

How to Use Reminders and Why Bother?

Just like tags, Evernote reminders are a feature that not everyone uses – or even thinks about using. By assigning reminders to specific notes, you can get a nudge on a specific date and time about the note. Whether you need to go to a meeting and the note contains directions or the note contains an outline to a section of your book that you need to begin, reminders can keep you accountable and on schedule.

Going back to the foodie / travel writer example: Imagine that you're meeting a Seattle chef on Friday. You can use reminders to attach a nudge to the main Seattle note within your Evernote account for Thursday. That way, the note will be brought to your attention a day in advance.

Once you get in the habit of using Evernote reminders to track deadlines on all of your projects, you don't have to worry about a deadline sneaking up on you. In one of my book projects for a traditional publisher, I had several interim deadlines, so adding notes with reminders was really useful.

Here's how to add a reminder: Click or tap on the alarm clock icon when you're in a note.

Screenshot 18: Reminders

Choose a due date, and Evernote will alert you of an upcoming reminder with:

> ➢ in-app notification
>
> ➢ email
>
> ➢ badge on the app tile

Once you've set a reminder for a note, it will appear at the top of your note list, and you can check it off once it's no longer a priority or has been accomplished. By the way, the desktop version of Evernote has an alarm clock icon and the word 'Reminder.'

If you want a daily digest of all the reminders you have set for each day, click the pull-down menu next to your name (upper right corner) and choose Account

Settings. On the next page, in the left column, you'll see
Reminders. Click it to bring up this screen:

Screenshot 19: Reminder notifications

Choose your time zone and check the Reminder Email
box to receive the daily digest.

SEARCH:
THE POWER OF SEARCH

One of the biggest advantages to keeping digital records – as opposed to physical ones – is the ease with which you can search those documents.

If you use Evernote to compile and store documents, notes, images, and more, you can search them quickly and easily. Instead of searching through a file cabinet or the top of your desk looking for the one piece of paper that has the information you need, just type a couple of keywords into the Evernote search box and the desired document will quickly be found. In this example, I've searched for 'marketing' with All Notes.

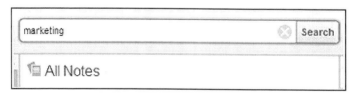

Screenshot 20: Searching

You can also search for a keyword within a specific notebook, like this example shows. Note that the search box now shows the name of the notebook within which I'm searching.

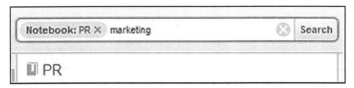

Screenshot 21: Searching within a notebook

If you're working on a book or another writing project, you're probably pulling in information from several sources, such as an RSS feed, a news item, a blog post, or online magazine article. Not only do you need to **save those sources** for later access, but you may have to cite them properly either at the end of your book, to a publisher's fact checker, or to your project manager.

Note: For my traditionally published books, it's common for the fact checker to email me asking for the source of something I've cited. Evernote is a life-saver.

Search is useful for finding all of the sources you used throughout your process, as long as you saved it within Evernote. Instead of wasting time looking for things, Evernote gives you the organizational tools to make it your "electronic secretary." Because I juggle so many clients and so many projects, without Evernote's organization I'd be swimming in (unorganized) paper.

Search Basics

The basic search function in Evernote is simple: Just type a keyword into the search bar at the top of the page and Evernote will find any notes containing that keyword or keywords.

Screenshot 22: Search within titles and content

Because Evernote searches both the title and the content of the note, the title of the note doesn't have to contain your keyword. Once the search is complete and you have a list of notes or articles containing that keyword, click on any of the articles to open it in the right window pane.

> Then they wake up. Peter McGraw, a marketing and psychology professor, and coauthor of the recently published book *The Humor Code*, says that an author friend warned him that "publishers print books and authors sell books. That was useful to have that perspective early on." Authors have to stand out in a crowded marketplace, and they're often footing their own marketing bills.

Screenshot 23: Keywords highlighted

If you scroll down through the article itself (right column), you'll see your keyword highlighted in yellow.

Most of the time a simple search will be all you'll need to do in order to find a note. However, there are some additional search tools that you can use when needed. More on that in just a second.

When you do a simple search, Evernote searches through your notebooks and returns all relevant items. As noted above, Search just doesn't look at titles or content, it also searches tags and text within images.

TEXT WITHIN IMAGES

This Evernote feature is amazing. Search will look for typed and (legibly) handwritten content and include those Search results. If you're one of those people who like to brainstorm with pen and paper, you can load those notes into Evernote and they'll be included in the Search. How cool is that?

UTILIZING SEARCH OPTIONS

As you continue to use Evernote for more and more projects, you'll begin amassing a huge assortment of notes and notebooks. If that's the case, search options are an effective way to narrow down your results so they're as relevant as possible. Designated search syntax allows you to search only within specific tags, notebooks, or other attributes.

For example, let's continue the 'cookie' idea from earlier. If you're writing a large cookbook, you might have hundreds of notes with the tag 'cookie' – so that filter alone won't help you much. Using a custom search option, you can start by searching within the tag 'cookie', but then narrow it down further by searching within the tag 'chocolate.'

Then, you can search for exactly the term you're trying to find, like low calorie. This search would yield all of your recipe notes relating to low calorie chocolate cookie recipes, without overwhelming you with unrelated results. Getting the exact note you need as quickly as possible is the goal of Evernote search, and the search options make that even easier.

One of my own tags is 'image size'. Because I tend to use a lot of images in my books and on my blog, it's a useful tag. In this search instance, I wanted to see what I have saved in Evernote about the image size recommended for a Kindle book.

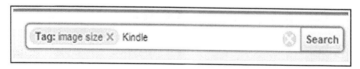

Screenshot 24: Regular searches

TYPE AHEAD SEARCH FINISHES YOUR THOUGHT

Google and Amazon have spoiled us with their "type ahead" feature. Whenever you start to type something into either of the Internet giants, they whirl their brain and automatically come up with the most frequently searched terms that begin with whatever word you typed:

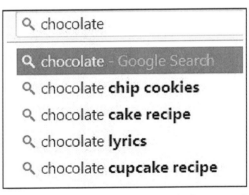

Screenshot 25: Evernote types ahead when searching

Evernote does the same thing, by attempting to finish your words and phrases. This is a useful feature for large notebooks that have thousands of entries.

You don't have to do anything special to use this feature – just start typing and Evernote will do the rest.

EVERNOTE PREMIUM

Evernote Premium members gain even more search power.

The basic search capability is more than enough power for the average user. However, if you have extremely large notebooks to sort through, or if you have a high number of attachments to your notes, this premium feature may be of interest to you.

When you have a premium Evernote account, the search function will actually look inside attached files and attempt to find your search terms. It will look inside scanned PDFs, and a variety of Microsoft Office and iWork file types including documents and spreadsheets. For someone who has attached a lot of files to their Evernote notebooks and needs to get specific information from them in a timely manner, this search features is a real time-saver.

When you're just getting started with Evernote, it might seem like you will never have enough notes to warrant using the search function – you can just open the right notebook and find all of your notes in plain sight. However, it won't take long before the notes start to pile up and the search function quickly becomes a vital part of your productivity.

However, as I said earlier – I've never reached the point of needing Premium Evernote – but your needs may far surpass my own.

Alert: Features You May Not Notice

SOURCE URLS

If you copy an image from the Web or nab text from a website, Evernote will capture the URL (website address) of the source. This is a great feature for those of us who occasionally need to cite our sources.

OCR

OCR (Optical Character Recognition) is a technology that's been around for a long time; however, it's far improved over its early days. Here's how it works: If you have a document and it's saved as an image, i.e. a .jpg file, Evernote can detect the text and make it searchable, even though it's an image. I scanned a page from one of my books (*Make Your Book Work Harder*) and then searched for one of the words within that image. Evernote found it in a split second.

GEOTAGS

If you're using Evernote on a mobile device, you can tag a note by location. If you're using Windows desktop you'll have to do this manually. Why would you want to geotag? If I'm traveling and take a photo with my phone, I want to be sure that exact location is captured – particularly if I'm in the back-of-beyond, which is often one of my destinations.

The screenshot below is from the iPhone. It shows a geotag and includes the name of the note and where I was when I created it. (Starbucks.)

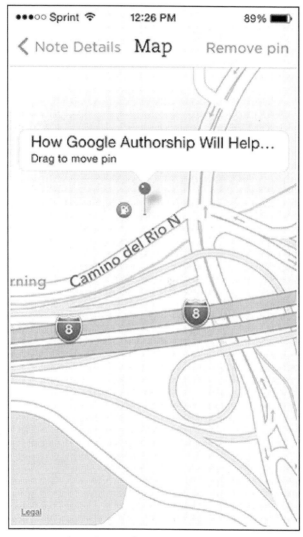

Screenshot 26: Geotags

Searching by GeoLocation

Remember all of the stuff I wrote about the power of Evernote search? One other way you can search for notes is by searching by GeoLocation. Currently, there are three ways to do a location search.

Here's how to search by location.

Evernote Atlas is available on Evernote for Mac and Evernote for Windows Desktop. Evernote Places is an app for iOS devices. If you're on your desktop version, select Atlas from the left column (it's towards the bottom of the column).

Screenshot 27: Atlas

Once you click on Atlas, a new window will open showing "cards" for each city, state and country where Evernote captured location information for your notes. Click a card and you'll next see a Google map showing your notes grouped by location, as well as the number of notes you created at that place. Click on the number shown on the map (see next image) and click to see all of the notes created at that location.

If you have an iOS device (iPhone, iPad, or iPod Touch), download the free Evernote Places app. You'll need to give the app permission to access your Evernote account. To search for notes by location, select Places from your home screen and tap a location pin on the map.

If you're using Evernote for Android, list all notes by

location and select the ones associated with a specific location. To generate the list, select Options > Sort.

Screenshot 28: Notes grouped by location

BETTER BROWSING WITH THE EVERNOTE CLIPPER

When working on any kind of writing project, browsing the Web is probably a big part of your creative or research process. Whether you're looking for concrete research for your book, or just want to spark some ideas, the Web is probably the first place you'll go.

As you browse the Web looking for inspiration or information, you may find long articles about your topic or little bits and pieces. If you had to bookmark and then return to each of those web pages it would take you a long time to compile all of the information you found.

Fortunately, you don't have to. Evernote (the people who seem to think of everything!) created a Web Clipper. This tool allows you to 'clip' pieces of web pages, whether it be text, images, links, etc., and save them into your Evernote account for later access.

These clippings are just like any other note in your Evernote account and can be sorted by tags, notebooks, etc. To maximize your web browsing time, as well as keep your writing and research organized, the Web Clipper is an invaluable tool.

WIDE-RANGING COMPATIBILITY

If you use any of the most-popular web browsers, you'll have no trouble putting the Web Clipper into action. Evernote offers this tool for:

- ➢ Chrome
- ➢ Firefox
- ➢ Safari
- ➢ Opera
- ➢ Internet Explorer

You can find the Evernote Clipper here:

http://evernote.com/webclipper

It's a browser extension so, depending on your browser, you may have to give it permission to install. When the extension is installed, you'll see the iconic elephant up in your browser toolbar.

Once you find a web page (or image, etc) that you want to save, click on the elephant and the Clipper panel will slide in from the right, exposing all the features from top to bottom.

Screenshot 29: Clipper panel

CLIPPER TOOLS

I'm going to go through each of the features of the Clipper panel because they are so useful I don't want you to miss out on any of them.

Clipping

At the top of the Clipper panel you'll see options to clip:

> ➢ article
>
> ➢ simplified article
>
> ➢ full page
>
> ➢ bookmark
>
> ➢ screenshot

ARTICLE

Will clip the body of the webpage, including links and images.

SIMPLIFIED ARTICLE

Strips away everything on the page except for the article. (This is my default choice.)

FULL PAGE

Exactly what you'd think – it grabs everything on the page, including ads.

BOOKMARK

Create a little snippet of the page along with the URL.

Screenshot 30: Bookmarks

SCREENSHOT

Takes a screenshot of the visible page (not the entire page), which you can then use with the Markup Tools (next image). The Markup Tools are the same tools you'll find in Skitch. I think it's really cool that Evernote added these to the Clipper because it saves having to take a picture, import it into Skitch, and then back into Evernote. This is an all-in-one solution.

Screenshot 31: Markup Tools

Markup Tools

LEFT COLUMN	RIGHT COLUMN
Highlighter	Marker
Arrow	Text tool
Stamp	Pixelator
Colors	Crop
Zoom out	Zoom in

You can use the Markup Tools on the screenshot or on any web page.

SHARE

Once you've captured the webpage (and done markup, as needed) you can share the page by clicking the Share button at the bottom of the Clipper panel via Facebook, Twitter, LinkedIn, or email.

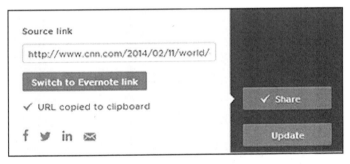

Screenshot 32: Share link

FILE

In the middle of the Clipper panel you'll see a section titled File. If you click on the name of the visible notebook, another panel will appear with the name of all of your notebooks. You can select whichever notebook you want to store the web clipping in, as well as add tags and comments.

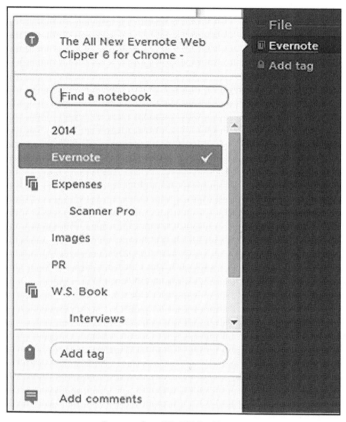

Screenshot 33: Web clipper

Why Not Just Use Bookmarks?

At first blush, you might just think it would be easier to bookmark the pages you want to save. After all, any web browser has a bookmark function, and it is easy enough to just click the bookmark button whenever you find something that you're interested in taking a closer look at later on. However, once you dig a little deeper, you will see that the web clipper goes well beyond any functionality that you're going to get from simply bookmarking a page.

To start with, web clippings are yours for as long as you need them – even if the webpage changes or goes away. This is a common problem that writers run into when doing research for a project. You might find something interesting, bookmark it into a specific folder, and leave it there for months – or even years. When you get around to the point in your project where that page will come in handy, the page may have been edited, or the website may have simply gone away. Then you have lost the ability to access that information and have to start looking again.

By using the Evernote web clipper, you can grab a piece of a page – or the whole thing – and save it to your Evernote account. Even if that page changes ten seconds after you take the clipping, your notes will be unaffected. It can sit in your Evernote account for as long as you like and will always be there when you need it.

Grab Only What You Need

With a bookmark, you're simply saving the URL of a given page so that you can return to it at a later date. By using the clipper, you can pull out only the information you're interested in and save it to Evernote. This way, when you look at your notes later on, you won't have to sift through the irrelevant information to get at what you need. Only the valuable part will have been saved. Yet another time-saver.

ORGANIZING CLIPS

Because clippings are just 'notes,' you can assign them to different notebooks and apply tags. As your writing project gets bigger and bigger, you're likely to find that the reference materials you saved are quickly adding up.

Sorting through all of the various web pages you've referenced can be a massive chore – unless all of those notes are neatly organized within Evernote. Whether you're sitting down for a focused research session, or you just happen upon something useful while you were casually surfing the web, it can be easily clipped and filed away in a matter of moments.

Always Accessible

If you have Evernote set up on your computer(s) as well as your mobile devices, you'll always be able to access your clippings wherever you happen to be. This kind of flexibility makes my writing and research chores way easier than if I had to be at my own desktop computer in order to get any work done.

EVERNOTE MOBILE

I love Evernote on my iPhone and iPad probably as much as you love yours on the Android. I'm a photo junkie and do my best to find ways of integrating photos I snap with the iPhone into a project. By shooting an image from within Evernote, I can save it directly in the relevant notebook.

The same is true with making audio notes; but instead of using my phone's built-in recorder and then uploading it, I create a voice-to-text note from within Evernote using the iPhone's built-in mic.

Available Across All Devices

No matter what kind of mobile device you love to use, I'm pretty sure Evernote offers an app. This makes it easy to connect all of your notes and notebooks via synch. Android, iPhone, iPad, Windows Phone, and even Blackberry are all supported.

While it isn't surprising that a powerful program like Evernote is available on all different kinds of devices, that is a feature that sets it apart from some other programs and services. Even if you only use one type of device at the moment, you never know what the future will bring – and what a relief to know that Evernote can follow you even if you make the switch from Android to iPhone or vice versa.

Make It Fit Your Needs

Depending on the type of writing or work that you do, your Evernote needs are going to be different from mine. One of the greatest assets of the system is its versatility. The mobile apps (discussed a bit later) provide countless features to be used – some of which you won't be interested in and others you'll use all the time. Once you download Evernote onto your mobile device and try mobile apps, you'll be hooked. (Have I said that before?)

Access Your Desktop Data

This is a huge one for me. I do not like being chained to my desktop computer, although it does have my entire life saved on it. But when I'm working on a project, I enjoy getting out to a coffeehouse and still being able to access references I need for a book or client project.

Since everything I've uploaded, clipped, or saved is in my Evernote account, I can grab any of them via my phone. Think about the upside of sitting with a client and being able to pull up some important piece of information about their project. Or, if I'm out doing research – like doing an interview or going to a museum or visitor center – I can grab information from my account, like directions to a museum or info about the person I'm interviewing.

Of course, because you can sync across devices, accessibility goes both ways. That means if you save something on your mobile device you can also see it on your Web-based Evernote or your desktop Evernote. Mobile notes can be anything from an idea that came into your head while you were out for a walk, to a conversation you had with someone in a meeting.

EVERNOTE FOR THE TRAVELING WRITER (OR TRAVEL WRITER)

It isn't easy to stay organized when planning a trip. My old way of putting together my trip information was to print pages and pages of websites for places I thought I might want to visit and then hole punch and add them to a three-ring binder that I took with me. Now, I use Evernote on my iPhone and iPad to stash everything about the places I'm going – from maps, to directions, hours of operation, rental car arrangements, plane tickets, hotel reservations, and interviews I've pre-arranged.

Having all of this information in one place is not only a time-saver but can be a life-saver when the hotel mysteriously loses my reservation.

If you're traveling for research, you can use Evernote to track business expenses. I scan receipts using the Scanner Pro app, then upload to Evernote. Scanner Pro will initially ask permission to access your Evernote account; once verified, you can pick which notebook you want to stash receipts and which tags to use. The scan is saved in PDF format, making it really easy to print (if necessary).

USING EVERNOTE TO PLAN A RESEARCH OR WRITING TRIP

Everyone loves going on vacation – even if it's a working one. Getting away from your desk and your usual routine is a great way to kick your creativity into high gear. No matter where you prefer to take your vacations, they're great for just getting your life back in balance – even if you spend part of your day doing business.

Depending on the type of trip you're taking, you may need to make airline reservations, hotel accommodations, rental car reservations, and more. Here's how I use Evernote for my working vacations.

Vacation Notebook

If you're already an Evernote user, open a new notebook dedicated to your upcoming trip. This will give you a good place to store everything that you collect related to your trip, including confirmation numbers, directions, itineraries, and more. As you browse the web looking for ideas of things to do while you're on the trip, you can use the Web Clipper to grab parts of web pages and save them to your notebook. This is where I use Stacks – as in Kansas Trip: Images, Reservations, Directions, Museums, and Interviews.

During the planning phase, make a note that includes a checklist of things you need to do before you go. Do you remember that you can create a checklist in a note? This can serve as a 'master list' from which you can work off of. When everything on the list has been checked, you'll know that all of the tasks are complete. If you hand-wrote your list on a piece of paper, you can still use Evernote; just snap a photo of the list and upload it to Evernote so you can access it long after the piece of paper has been thrown away.

Take Advantage of the Mobile Access

By downloading the Evernote mobile app onto your phone or tablet, you'll have access to all of your notes, assuming you have cell phone coverage! If you have made notes about restaurants you want to try, or what sights you want to see, just pull them up on your phone and you can keep the trip moving in the right direction.

Also, if you're taking pictures on your phone of landmarks, interview subjects, or inspirational views, save those into Evernote as well. When you get home, you can sort through all of the photos you took and just pick out your favorites for storage into your Evernote notebook.

MY RESEARCH ASSISTANT

It almost seems as if Evernote was designed for research. Its capabilities to store, share, and provide easy access to saved notes is a clue of its value to writers. Whether researching a fiction or non-fiction book, the Notebook-Note system really lends itself to the process. Read on to see my own process.

Creating Research Notebooks

I'm currently working on a new book about San Diego. I've never written a travel book before, but it's something I've always wanted to do – particularly about a city that I know so well.

I first decided on how I wanted to structure the book. San Diego is a very neighborhood-centric city. Each neighborhood has a unique character and many times neighborhoods have a central gathering hub – whether a Starbucks, corner grocery, or even neighborhood theatre.

Neighborhoods are so central to getting around San Diego that many even have their own signage across the main street into the neighborhood.

Screenshot 34: Photos for travel writing

The reason you see a Trolley Car on the University Heights sign is because the trolley barn (where trolleys spent the night back in the day) was once a part of this old neighborhood. *(By the way, if you're ever in University Heights, go to Lestat's on Park – my favorite coffee house.)*

I knew that my book was going to be organized by neighborhood and include tips about great eateries or coffee houses in each area – and things to avoid: like trying to get a parking space in Balboa Park on a beautiful Sunday!

I also knew that I was going to have to do a little research into each neighborhood. Fortunately, I authored the coffee table book *San Diego Then and Now[3]*, so I had some history but not all. Of course, I'll also need photographs, many of which I already have, but some that I found (copyright-free) online.

Based on how I want to set up my book, I created this Notebook-Stack system within my Evernote account:

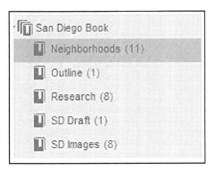

Screenshot 35: Notebook stacking example

As you can see, I created a notebook for the many neighborhoods I want to include, as well as ones for my outline, my draft, research, and images. Now, when I'm online researching neighborhoods, San Diego history, or hunting down images, I can use the Web Clipper to move them directly into the relevant notebook.

By the way – if you're searching for online images you can either use the Web Clipper to grab the page, or you can right-click an image. One of your choices will be Clip image – and once you hover over that, a second box will open giving you more options – and of course I picked the Evernote Web Clipper.

---

[3] http://www.amazon.com/San-Diego-Then-Nancy-Hendrickson/dp/1592231268

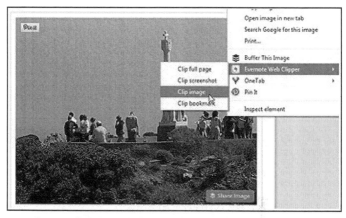

Screenshot 36: Saving an image using the web clipper

I personally use the right-click when saving images. Once you do the right-click save, a last box will appear, letting you know that the image was saved into Evernote. As you can see, it also tells you the name of the website.

Screenshot 37: Clipped image with source site

If you click over to your Evernote account, you'll see that the original link to the image is also saved.

Did you notice in the Clipped to Evernote screenshot that once saved you can also share on LinkedIn, Facebook, Twitter, via email, and via a link?

I never save via a link because who knows when this site or this image might disappear.

A GENTLE REMINDER ABOUT MOVING WEB CLIPS INTO NOTEBOOKS

Just to refresh your memory: Evernote Web Clipper is a utility that allows the capturing and saving of snapshots of web pages.

The good thing here is that image, texts, tags, and other elements on a webpage are all preserved when saved in a notebook. Putting web clips into your notebooks would differ a bit for every type of device used, but just for drill, here's how to pull a web page into Evernote using your browser.

EVERNOTE WEB CLIPPING USING A PC/WEB-BASED BROWSER

For Chrome users, the first thing to do is to install the Evernote Web Clipper App. The Chrome App Store makes this available for free. If you can't find it, go to the Chrome store[4] and do a search.

---

[4] https://chrome.google.com/webstore/category/apps

Once the app has been installed on your browser, the Evernote icon will appear on the browser toolbar.

Screenshot 38: Evernote icon in browser toolbar

Every time the icon is clicked, a sidebar will appear. Options such as Clip, Markup, and File will be there. (Refer back to those chapters for detailed information.)

COLLABORATIVE WRITING

I've co-authored four books and really appreciate any technology that can make collaborative writing easier. Of course sharing a notebook is a start, but another solution is an app called LiveMinutes[5]. It's free to use and integrates seamlessly with your Evernote account.

The concept is simple. LiveMinutes creates a shared workspace for anyone working on the project. Its features include teleconferencing with video chat and IM. Any notes uploaded can be accessed and edited by each writer and the saved notes are immediately available for any other team members. (Think virtual assistant.)

Once you've set up your LiveMinutes account, go to Settings to integrate Evernote. LiveMinutes now let's you open your Evernote notes in projects and edit them. Then, it saves back all notes created or edited back to Evernote in a 'LiveMinutes' notebook.

---

[5] http://liveminutes.com/

The integration of LiveMinutes to Evernote creates a smooth means of collaboration between researchers or writers. New members of the team who have joined the workspace and have no copies of those notes don't need to worry. Copies are available on their LiveMinutes notebook after access to a shared notebook has been established. As each member of the team edits and saves each note, the local and shared notebook copies are also updated.

Caveat: Only up to 5 workspaces are free of charge. Exceeding this involves a monthly charge.

THE ELEPHANT'S TRUNK

You just have to appreciate the people over at Evernote – they definitely have a sense of humor. It's apparent by the name they gave their extensive App Center – the Trunk. This is where you'll find a complete collection of applications. As Evernote says, you'll also find hardware and software products "providing everything from business card scanning to expense management to simply creating better memories — and they all work with Evernote."

You'll find the App Center here:

https://appcenter.evernote.com

Select your platform by clicking on one of the choices in the box at the App Center:

Screenshot 39: App Center

Depending on your platform, you'll see a range of different apps for your particular platform. This is a screenshot of a *partial* list of apps:

Screenshot 40: Some apps (there are lots!)

Select an app to read more about it – then click the Install button. The screenshot here is for the installation of Clarify.

Screenshot 41: Clarify app

Per the description, "Clarify is screen capture software for Mac and Windows that lets you export multiple images from your Evernote account into a document where they're automatically organized in sequence. Clarify is great for creating process documentation or how-to's. Once your document is created, you can export the entire document with multiple images directly to your Evernote account for future reference."

As you get comfortable using Evernote on a regular basis, you may want to explore some of these extra apps and features. The specific apps that will be most-beneficial to you depends on how you use Evernote and what kind of projects you're working on. These apps are installed on your iPhone or Android device just like any other, and they integrate nicely with Evernote to provide you with even more capabilities.

Below is a list of a few Evernote apps that will be of particular interest to authors.

CamScanner – Android and iPhone

The CamScanner app is both simple and amazing all at the same time. It allows you to use the camera on your mobile device as a scanner by taking an image and making the text easier to read. Once it has done its work, the resulting document can be exported straight to your Evernote account for storage. Instead of just taking basic pictures of your notes and trying to get them just right so you can read the writing, CamScanner does most of the hard work for you.

Benefits for this app for an author are obvious. Most writers like to make physical notes during the writing process and saving those into Evernote can help you be more organized and make sure you don't lose track of any of your best thoughts or ideas. Before that pile of hand-written notes gets out of control, use CamScanner to capture them and file them away in the proper Evernote location. When the time comes to review your ideas, the note will be right where you left it – even if you have long since thrown away the actual paper copy.

Scanner Pro – Android and iPhone

I've used CamScanner and Scanner Pro, and they're both excellent. I tend to use Scanner Pro more – don't ask me why; just personal preference.

Like CamScanner, this app is great for scanning receipts or documents when I'm on the road. The app optimizes the image as well as squaring off the corners.

Once I'm satisfied with the end result, all I have to do is tell it to go to Evernote.

By the way, once you connect your Scanner Pro with Evernote, you'll get an email from Evernote telling you that the two things are now connected.

cleverList – iOS 5.1 or later

List-making apps can come in handy for a variety of tasks – everything from working on your book project to simply going to the grocery store. The problem with most list-making apps is that they stand alone and don't integrate with your other organizational tools. That is not the case with cleverList. This app provides a quick and easy way to make a list or note which can then be synchronized with Evernote. You can place your notes into specific notebooks just as with everything in Evernote, so you can always find old lists when you need them.

As an author, you can use this list app for outlining ideas you have for specific chapters or scenes. No matter when your ideas hit you, simply pull out your mobile iOS device and fill in a note. Once filed into Evernote, you can call on it later when you're ready to begin writing. cleverList is simple and easy to use, yet incredibly powerful for capturing your ideas.

SpeakToIt Assistant - Android

Sometimes, you just aren't able to type out a message to yourself that you can save into Evernote. With this app, you can enter a quick note without even picking up the phone. SpeakToIt Assistant is a handy app that allows you to dictate audio notes which are then saved right into Evernote for you to view later. Whenever something pops into your head, you can just dictate the thought into your phone, and it will land neatly in your Evernote account.

This is another app that has obvious benefits for authors. Ideas are fickle in when they come about so being able to record them and file them away is a huge bonus. There might not be anything more frustrating when working on a writing project then having a great idea get away because you never got the chance to record it while it was fresh in your mind. Not only does SpeakToIt Assistant make it easy to record your thoughts, it also makes it easy to organize them thanks to automatic syncing with Evernote.

FastEver Snap – iOS

This app costs $1.99 and it's one I use all the time, probably because I take so many pictures - - they really are my inspiration.

FastEver Snap opens the camera, you snap the shot, and then it's sent directly to Evernote. You can resize the photos before you upload in order to limit the upload size. In addition, you can add tags and specify which notebook the photo should be moved to.

FEATURES INCLUDE:

- ➢ Fast activation
- ➢ Image sizes are compressed for sending small file sizes
- ➢ You can choose image sizes from original size, UXGA(1600 × 1200), XGA(1024 × 768), VGA (640 × 480) and QVGA (320 × 240). (Default is XGA.)
- ➢ Supports notebook and tags
- ➢ Supports title entry
- ➢ Auto geolocation tagging
- ➢ Saves photos in queue when offline
- ➢ Background transmission with multitask
- ➢ Digital zoom & touch focus
- ➢ Option to save original photos in camera roll
- ➢ Grid display option
- ➢ Volume shutter
- ➢ Option to turn preview on/off

News360 – Android and iOS

Not all Evernote apps have to do with storing your notes or ideas for later. The News360 app makes it easier for you to keep up to date on all of the relevant issues going on in the world around you. By ~~snooping~~ analyzing your Evernote account, this app can learn about your interests and then tailor the feed for you. Information is gathered from 10,000 sources. Those articles can be saved right back into your Evernote account, so you will know where to look for them when you have time to read.

In reality, you don't need to use any additional apps to get a great experience from Evernote. However, if you do decide to employ some of these apps, you can get even more use from your Evernote account and discover even more ways to be productive. The apps listed above are just a sample of what is available in both the Google Play Store and the Apple App Store, so make sure to browse around and see if there is an app that exactly suits your needs and can enhance the benefits that you get from using Evernote.

A Perfect Marriage – Evernote And Twitter

Dum-dum-da-dum, dum-dum, da-dum…

You already know how powerful of a tool Evernote can be for an author (or anyone, for that matter). Working on a writing project of any kind is a huge undertaking, and Evernote makes it easier than ever before to stay organized and make sure that none of your notes or ideas get lost in the shuffle.

The same can be said of Twitter. In terms of gathering information from a wide range of sources, Twitter is hard to beat. It seems that anybody who is anybody has a Twitter account, and the platform is extremely easy to search – meaning you can find information that is relevant to your project quickly. Whether you gather ideas by following specific people or just searching specific terms periodically, there is tons of information to be had just by spending some time on Twitter each day.

Naturally, then, it makes sense to marry Twitter and Evernote to take advantage of the strengths of each platform. Twitter is a great way to gather large amounts of information, and Evernote is a great way to organize and store information. A match made in heaven? Hmmm.

PREPARING FOR THE WEDDING

First, you'll need both an Evernote and Twitter account. By this point, you probably already have Evernote set up on your computer and mobile devices, so it's time to create a Twitter handle if you don't already have one. It's okay if you don't even plan on sending out a single tweet – you can gather tons of information without actively posting anything.

Head to Twitter.com and register your '@name.' It's free and shouldn't take more than thirty seconds to sign up. Once registered, you can start to follow some people and get familiar with the site. If you're currently working on a specific writing project within a certain field or niche, it would be wise to follow some people who are influential within that field – you never know what kind of valuable information is floating through the Twitterverse.

Something neat about Twitter is its interconnected nature. You may start out by looking at tweets from one account and wind your way to several other relevant accounts.

CONNECTING TO EVERNOTE

There are a few ways to funnel tweets into Evernote, but IFTTT[6].com is one of the most-popular and most-useful. I've written more on how to use IFTTT.com with Evernote a little later. For now, though, there are two specific ways that IFTTT can be useful for saving Tweets.

Saving all of your tweets

Using IFTTT, it is possible to set up a 'recipe' that will archive all of your tweets and send them to Evernote for archiving.

Saving favorite tweets

This function is more useful for people who use Twitter passively to discover information, rather than tweet it out to their followers. Once the recipe is set up, you can simply save all tweets that you mark as 'favorites' into Evernote so you can look at them later. In this way, your IFTTT recipe can kind of work like the web clipper feature on Evernote – grabbing individual tweets that you like and storing them.

---

[6] http://ifttt.com/

HOW THE MARRIAGE CAN HELP YOU, THE AUTHOR

Sure, it's cool to hook up your Evernote and Twitter accounts but what's the big deal?

Browsing Twitter looking for information related to your project can be a bit of a drudge – and something that I, personally, don't particularly enjoy. However, quickly finding and sending the information to Evernote makes this marriage far more attractive to me. Now, instead of following all the links within tweets, simply save them into Evernote, then later, when you need to get serious about your project, you can go back and select the tweets that really have the valuable information (links).

Twitter is an especially useful resource for an author if you're working on a piece that is time-sensitive. Twitter reacts to breaking news faster than any other medium so keeping your eye on the trending topics is a great way to spot information quickly.

Finally – and this is a biggie – it's the best social network (in my opinion) to find experts within a certain field. And, it's easy to communicate with them and begin building a working relationship. You might be surprised at how many well-known people are willing to lend a hand.

USING IFTTT.COM RECIPES FOR EVERNOTE

Most authors use a variety of web-based services to keep track of their lives: personal, social, and business. Whether it's your social media accounts like Facebook and Twitter or productivity accounts like Evernote, there's a lot to keep track of. IFTTT is one of those free services that makes my life far easier – plus (and this is a real plus), it easily connects several services to your Evernote account.

IFTTT Basics

IFTTT, which stands for 'if this, then that,' is a service that helps you to connect an incredible number of services and accounts, known as 'channels.' The channels are connected through specific 'recipes' that dictate what kind of action the service takes when prompted. While it might sound complicated at first, it is, in fact, quite simple and very convenient once you get the hang of it.

Example: If I post an image to Instagram then I also post that image to a specific folder on Evernote.

There are currently 116 channels, including Facebook, Twitter, LinkedIn, Gmail, Pinterest, Instagram, YouTube, WordPress, and many more. Once you 'activate' a channel (by logging into the channel), you can create your own recipes. However, I've yet to create my own recipe because there are hundreds already created.

Why I Love This Service

Basically, IFTTT allows me to send information from one of my accounts to another, automatically. This will occur when one of my recipes is triggered by a specific action on one channel, which then directs information to another channel.

Another example:

> Imagine that you use Facebook as a method of promoting your writing business and your book sales. As an author, it's vital that you communicate with your audience and stay in touch with them as much as possible – and Facebook is one of the best possible ways to do just that. Instead of having Facebook comments that involve you and your books slip through the cracks, you can set up an IFTTT recipe that routes all of them into Evernote. That way, any time you're mentioned on Facebook, an action will be

triggered that sends a note into your Evernote account. For someone who spends all day on Evernote, but might only check Facebook periodically, this can be a great benefit.

This is just but one of many examples of how IFTTT can be used to keep track of your online life and have activity directed toward the channel that you use the most. As a result, you can have more timely responses to messages or other actions, all while not having to check each of your accounts all day long.

Evernote - IFTTT Recipes You'll Love

For the purposes of this book, we need to track down IFTTT recipes that relate to Evernote and can be helpful for authors working on projects. Assuming you're using Evernote as your main method of staying organized and on track with your project, these recipes will help you by routing information into Evernote that you can use later on.

Following are a few ideas for recipes that could be specifically useful in your writing endeavors.

SAVE STARRED EMAILS TO EVERNOTE

If you communicate with other writers, or interview subjects or clients via email, this recipe makes it easy to organize your important emails into a specific Evernote notebook. Once in place, all you need to do is click the 'star' button on any email within your Gmail account, and that email (along with the first attachment) will go into Evernote as a new note. For someone who gets a lot of email, this recipe can make a big difference by making it easier to sort through and pull out just what is important.

ARCHIVE INSTAGRAM PHOTOS INTO EVERNOTE

For the author who leans heavily on images in their work, this recipe can make sure your photos land right where you will see them on a regular basis.

Any time you post a new photo onto your Instagram account, it will automatically be saved in Evernote as a new image note.

SAVE FACEBOOK STATUS UPDATES

Posting on Facebook on a regular basis is a good idea for an author trying to grow a following, but it can be hard to keep track of everything that you have posted as the months (and years) go by. Using an IFTTT recipe, you can automatically save all of your Facebook updates into an Evernote notebook.

There is also a similar recipe that can be used for Twitter, so you can save all of your tweets in much the same way.

DROPBOX CONNECTION

If you use Dropbox along with Evernote, getting the two to work together can be a big time saver. There are recipes available which work in both directions – sending information from Evernote to Dropbox and vice versa.

This kind of recipe is one that you might not need as often, but it can really come in handy when you do.

SIRI TO EVERNOTE

This is one I frequently use because I talk to Siri so often. Once you activate this recipe (you'll have to download the iOS IFTTT app and you'll need to create a reminder list titled Evernote) you can talk to Siri and your note will be added to your Evernote account.

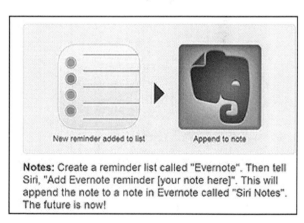

Screenshot 42: Siri to Evernote

It can be a little bit intimidating to get started on IFTTT.com if you aren't familiar with the concept at first. However, it is worth your time to get familiar with what it can do and how it can help you as a writer.

But why make it hard when I've already written a free step-by-step guide on using IFTTT. Do you remember at the beginning of the book that I offered you a free thank-you gift? In case you forgot:

IFTTT Made Easy for You

In case you didn't already grab this, I'd like to give you a step-by-step guide to IFTTT.com – a site that allows you (for free) to set up a "domino effect" social media marketing plan with ease.

http://nancyhendrickson.com/free

ONE-CLICK MARKETING FOR WRITERS

NANCY HENDRICKSON

I call it One-Click Marketing because you really can post book promotions on multiple sites, all from a single post or image.

Here's one what reader emailed me:

> *"I first ran across IFTTT in a blog on Sunday. Went to the site. Yikes! Thought another shorthand communication system that I can't understand. Then I downloaded your guide. You validated the whole IFTTT concept. Thank you!!"*

> Jeff Ezell

USING EVERNOTE WITH MOLESKINE® AND POST-IT NOTES®

I didn't want to finish out this section of the book without mentioning the use of Evernote, Moleskin, and Post-it Notes.

It isn't very often that the physical world comes together with the digital world in a successful way. Usually, you have to do all of your work on paper, or all on the computer, without the two really ever connecting. That's changed thanks to the technology that Evernote offers through the use of Moleskine notebooks and Post-it notes.

By using one or both of these methods to capture your notes, you can take your real-world writing and turn it into a searchable, saved note within your Evernote account.

No matter how high tech the world gets, some jobs are just done best with a pencil (or pen) and paper. If you like to work on your writing projects by first jotting down notes on paper, this compatibility was meant to make your life easier. You will be able to harness the power of Evernote while still being able to work the 'old-fashioned' way.

Moleskine Notebooks

Evernote offers a specific line of Moleskine brand notebooks that are designed specifically to be compatible with the document camera.

You can use the notebook just as you would any other – making drawings, take notes in a meeting, etc. – and then snap pictures of each page for automatic loading into Evernote notes.

Incredibly, the Evernote software is able to recognize handwriting text so you can actually search through your written notes once they're uploaded.

Don't worry about losing the physical copy of your notes because they will be saved in your Evernote account to be reviewed whenever necessary.

One of the most-impressive features of these Moleskine notebooks are the smart stickers that can be used for tagging. Just by placing specific stickers on certain pages of your notes, those notes will be tagged automatically to correlate with the sticker that was used. You won't even have to go into the note and add which tags you want to attach to it – the work will be done for you, thanks to the smart stickers.

Additionally, purchasing a notebook through Evernote will give you limited-time use of the premium version of Evernote. If you have been wanting to try out the premium features but weren't sure if you needed them, this is a good way to test it out while getting a great notebook at the same time. Depending on which notebook you purchase, the premium access will last between one and three months.

Prices may vary but expect to pay about $25 for 2 packages.

Post-it Notes

For shorter, yet still important, notes, Post-it notes are always useful. Now, with the help of Evernote, they can be ever more-useful than ever before. Just as with the Moleskine notebooks, you can snap a photo of your  Post-it notes and load them into Evernote to be organized and searched just like the rest of your notes.

Evernote offers a variety of Post-it note pads, all of which can be photographed to exactly replicate your original note. The Post-it notes come in four main colors, each of which can be tagged within Evernote. Then, when you take a picture of a note in a certain color, it will automatically be tagged appropriately without any further action on your end.

Not only are they available in the traditional standard size, but they are also offered in 'Big Pad' size so you can fit more important information into a single note. A single pad of 90 Post-it Notes currently sells for close to $16.

You might have reservations about using Evernote to transfer your handwritten notes into digital content – until you try it and experience first-hand just how well it works. No longer do you have to choose between hand-written and digital notes.

Whether you use the Moleskine notebooks, the Post-it notes, or both, putting written content into your Evernote account is a simple and streamlined process. As a long-time handwritten note-taker, I'm a big fan of Evernote Moleskines.

EVERNOTE FOR BUSINESS AND SCHOOL (BECAUSE THEY WRITE TOO)

If you're in the business world or in school, chances are you, too, have to write *something*: a report, a term paper, or a project update. This section of Evernote applies to you – the more casual writer.

USING EVERNOTE IN THE OFFICE

Evernote is so versatile it can be used in almost any setting, including the office. If you need to track time on a project, do research on best practices in your industry, or write interoffice or outgoing letters, you'll find that Evernote speeds up your process and your productivity.

Meeting Notes and Your Calendar

Do you need a personal planner that you can use for managing day-to-day business activities like keeping a project on track or keeping you on track?

By taking advantage of the Reminders feature on Evernote, you can take notes for meetings then set up a reminder for any action items.

As your meetings increase (don't they always!) and your calendar fills up, those action item Reminders can be a life-saver. I don't know about you, but I've let a few tasks slip out of my memory more than once.

Here's how you can best use Evernote as a meeting notes organizer: Take notes within Evernote while you're in the meeting, then (before it slips YOUR mind) set up a Reminder for any actionable items, next meetings, outcomes, or the contacts who require a follow-up.

If you work in a team, don't forget to check out Evernote productivity or business apps like Azendoo that is built for team collaboration and communication. Platforms currently available are iPhone, iPad, Android, Android Tablet, and Web.

You'll need to sign up for an Azendoo account, with pricing ranging from free to $9 a month.

Features include:

> ➤ Ability to share your Evernote notes into Azendoo discussions and tasks.

> ➤ Turn Evernote checkboxes into actionable Azendoo tasks, and syncing them both ways.

> ➤ Import Evernote task lists as Azendoo project templates.

> ➤ Save Azendoo task lists to Evernote.

> ➤ Evernote and Teams

If you work at a management level, one of your roles might be that of a project manager. As you know, if one or two people fall behind on project tasks, it can impact the entire project. Evernote can keep all of the tasks and information for each employee in one place.

Here's the process: Set up a different notebook within Evernote for each of your team, then share that notebook with them. When you have a new task or assignment to send their way, just add the details in a new note within the notebook. They will then have access to the note and can make changes or update you on their progress right within the note.

Instead of sending endless emails back and forth regarding a single project, you can manage it easily within Evernote.

The more team members you have to manage, the more Evernote can help keep order in your life. It can be far easier to manage a collection of notebooks of team members and their tasks as opposed to tracking down all of the back-and-forth emails regarding the project.

Notebooks can be shared with multiple people, as needed, so that team members have access only to the notebooks the team leader deems necessary.

Tracking Your Progress

No matter what business goals you're trying to reach, tracking your progress keeps you on top of your projects. You can use Evernote to set up goals within notebooks and edit your notes to reflect new goals, a change in direction, or new assets. By using Evernote as your consolidated organizational tool, everything you need to see will be right at your fingertips.

If you're as busy as most business people, Evernote can be a huge help. Once you settle on a system that best utilizes Evernote's features and your needs, you'll quickly see the power inherent in this service.

Take the time to create a system of notebooks that logically organize your business life and supports you working far more productively.

EVERNOTE GOES TO SCHOOL

As a student, you have more than enough on your plate. You probably have several classes to attend on a daily basis, homework to complete, and possibly a part-time job to work as well.

Anything you can do to stay organized and make sure you're working as efficiently as possible is a good thing. Using Evernote to stay on top of all of your studies is a great idea and could help you form habits that carry over into the working world when your school days are over.

Some of the features of Evernote are perfect for students who need to keep track of coursework in several different classes. Following are three parts of Evernote that should be of particular use to students.

Notebooks

One of the most-simple features in Evernote is the ability to create separate notebooks, but it is perfect for a student to take advantage of. By just setting up a notebook for each of your classes, you can make sure all of your notes and assignments end up in the same place. That way, there are no worries about finding the right paperwork or remembering to do your homework – keep everything in Evernote within the correct notebook and it will be there when you looking for it.

A great habit to get into is simply opening a new note within a notebook each time you're given an assignment. You can give that note a reminder for the day before the assignment is due, so you have time to finish it up before turning it in. No longer do you have to go to class and hope you haven't forgotten to do some of your work – as long as everything is entered into Evernote, you will be on top of it.

Image Capture

If you sit in class and take notes the 'old fashioned' way – i.e. with a pen and paper – you will want to get those notes into Evernote to stay organized. That process is quick and easy with image capture. All you need to do is take a picture of your notes with your phone and load them up into your Evernote account. You can then tag and place them into the right notebooks for easy retrieval later.

As long as you use good handwriting when you're taking your notes, you should be able to find words within your written notes using the Evernote search feature. This is a powerful capability and one of the best reasons to load all of your notes after you take them. Instead of sorting through page after page to find something specific, just search it, and Evernote will return all of the relevant results.

Web Clipper

If you're a student, you spend a lot of time on the web doing research for class assignments and projects. Use the Web Clipper feature from Evernote to grab pieces of web pages and store them into notes so you can reference them anytime you want.

Instead of just bookmarking interesting pages, the Web Clipper lets you save only what you need and file it away where you want it. Web pages are constantly changing, so using this feature lets you grab what you need and have it even long after the website has changed its content. Just download the Web Clipper into the browser of your choice and use it anytime you come across interesting content that could be helpful for a class project.

Usually, an organized student is a successful one. If you hope to excel in your classes and get the most from your educational experience, staying organized should be one of your primary goals. Evernote makes that easier than ever, so get started organizing your academic life using this amazing service.

CONCLUSION

I'm a big fan of actionable takeaways – and these are a few thoughts on what you can do next, now that you have a good understanding of how Evernote works:

Make a Daily Summary note (text or audio or video) of your writing or project goals. I didn't use to do this but I learned that making this kind of list before I go to bed does a couple of things: a) it helps me do a brain dump and I sleep better; and b) it reminds me of all that I accomplished – even on days when it feels like I didn't do anything.

Go through your browser bookmarks and see how many you really use. Take the ones that are your all-stars and get them out of bookmarks and into Evernote. For example, I have a looonnngggg list of bookmarks of sites where I can find copyright-free images. I pulled everyone of them out of bookmarks and into Evernote – now I know exactly where they are and can easily re-access them when needed.

If you're browsing a magazine and find a great article, snap its picture with your digital device, then send it over to Evernote. Remember – Evernote can search words within images.

I'd love to know other uses you discover for using Evernote. If this book is like everything else I've ever written, I'll be putting together a second edition in the next few months. And of course, I'd love to quote you and link to your website or your book – so let me know at: **nancy@nancyhendrickson.com**

DID YOU LIKE HOW TO USE EVERNOTE FOR WRITING AND RESEARCH?

Before you go, I'd like to say "Thanks" for purchasing this book. I know you have a huge selection of Kindle books from which to choose but you took a chance with me. So big thanks for downloading and reading all the way to the end.

I'd like to ask you for a *small* favor. If you found this book to be of benefit, would you please take a minute to leave a review on Amazon.

Your feedback helps me continue to write these books.

More Books by Nancy Hendrickson

If you found this book helpful, you may be interested in some of my other books for writers and bloggers:

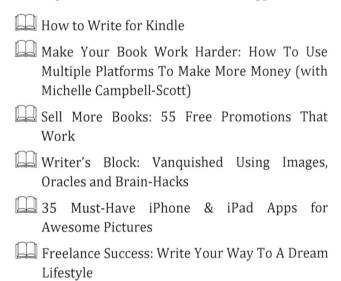 How to Write for Kindle

Make Your Book Work Harder: How To Use Multiple Platforms To Make More Money (with Michelle Campbell-Scott)

Sell More Books: 55 Free Promotions That Work

Writer's Block: Vanquished Using Images, Oracles and Brain-Hacks

35 Must-Have iPhone & iPad Apps for Awesome Pictures

Freelance Success: Write Your Way To A Dream Lifestyle

Facebook Page

I have had so much support for my writing that I'd like to support you in your work. I created a Facebook Page called Writer's Life - and would love for you to join me.

I frequently post about writing news, tips, great articles, and book sales ideas. I invite you to join me and welcome your comments, questions, and ideas.

You'll find me here:

https://www.facebook.com/writerslife

Of Course I Had to Have a P.S.

If you've found some great for using Evernote, email me at: nancy@nancyhendrickson.com and let me know if I can include it in the next edition of this book. Include, too, the link you'd like me to use to your website, blog or book.

Thank you!

INDEX

O

P

R

S

T

34961454R00080

Made in the USA
Lexington, KY
25 August 2014